WORKBOOK COMPANION FOR

THE FULL ARMOR OF GO[D]

ARE YOU SURE YOU GOT [IT?]

CRISTA CRAWFORD

P

Planted in Him

Publisher

O'Fallon, Illinois

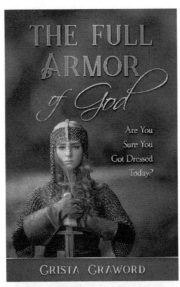

Let's Stay Connected!

Website: cristacrawford.com
Facebook: facebook.com/CCrawfordAuthor
Twitter: @CCrawfordAuthor
Instagram: instagram.com/ccrawfordauthor
Goodreads: bit.ly/cristacrawford

GROUP BIBLE STUDY
SPECIAL PRICING

The Armor of God

+

The Workbook Companion for The Armor of God

Please contact me here:

cristacrawford.com/contact

NEWSLETTER

Sign up to receive a *once a month* newsletter full of updates on new book releases, giveaways, discounts, and encouragement.

Sign up here:

cristacrawford.com/newsletter

CHRISTIAN AUTHOR AND SPEAKER

Copyright © 2018 Crista Crawford

Second Edition

All rights reserved. This book or parts thereof may not be reproduced in
any form, stored in any retrieval system, or transmitted in any form by
any means—graphic, electronic, mechanical, photocopy, recording, or
otherwise—without prior written permission of the author,
except in the case of brief quotations embodied in
critical articles and reviews.

Scripture quotations marked (NIV) are taken from the Holy Bible, New International
Version®, NIV®. Copyright © 1973, 1978, 1984, 2011 by Biblica, Inc.™ Used by
permission of Zondervan. All rights reserved worldwide. www.zondervan.com The "NIV"
and "New International Version" are trademarks registered in the United States Patent and
Trademark Office by Biblica, Inc.™

Scripture taken from the New King James Version®. Copyright © 1982 by Thomas Nelson.
Used by permission. All rights reserved.

Scripture quotations marked NLT are taken from the *Holy Bible*, New Living Translation,
copyright © 1996, 2004, 2015 by Tyndale House Foundation. Used by permission of Tyndale
House Publishers, Inc., Carol Stream, Illinois 60188. All rights reserved.

Scripture quotations marked ESV are from the ESV® Bible (The Holy Bible, English
Standard Version®), copyright © 2001 by Crossway, a publishing ministry of Good News
Publishers. Used by permission. All rights reserved.

Scriptures marked KJV are taken from the KING JAMES VERSION (KJV): KING JAMES
VERSION, public domain.

Scripture quotations marked NASB are taken from the New American Standard Bible®
(NASB), Copyright © 1960, 1962, 1963, 1968, 1971, 1972, 1973,1975, 1977, 1995 by The
Lockman Foundation. Used by permission. www.Lockman.org

Scripture quotations marked CSB®, are taken from the Christian Standard Bible®, Copyright
© 2017 by Holman Bible Publishers. Used by permission. Christian Standard Bible®, and
CSB® are federally registered trademarks of Holman Bible Publishers.

Any people depicted in stock imagery provided by Shutterstock are models,
and such images are being used for illustrative purposes only.
Certain stock imagery © Shutterstock.

ISBN: 978-0-9995407-5-6 (soft cover)

www.cristacrawford.com

CONTENTS

ACKNOWLEDGEMENTS

I would like to thank our children—through blood and lifelong friendship—for drawing the wonderful illustrations of each piece of armor. I admire your artistic talents and the special gifts God granted each one of you. Thank you (from oldest to youngest) Kimmra, Ashley, Mallory, Maddie, Bella, Kelsey, and Abby for using your gifts for His Glory.

Dear Fellow Armor Seeker,

How often do you take time out of your busy schedule to sit still, reflect, and listen to what God is trying to say to you? It's a real luxury, isn't it? God asks us to spend time with Him because He intimately knows it's the only way to replenish our tired and worn out bodies and spirits. I hope the questions in this workbook give you the opportunity to sit quietly with your Father.

As I wrote these questions, I found myself deeply reflecting on the questions I needed answered to grow in my awareness of Christ's armor before I was willing to wear it. Prayerfully, they will assist you on your journey towards walking daily in Christ's protection.

The first chapter of *The Full Armor of God: Are You Sure You Got Dressed Today?* opens with my life spinning out of control. This is the pre-armor wearing Crista whom I would love to put my arm around and say, *I know something you may need.* Picture my arm around you as you read and reflect. I never want you to feel my isolation by making the decision to go headlong into your struggles without the armor of God. He has much bigger plans for your life, and they do not include circumstances ruling over your peace and joy.

Think of a time, whether past or present, you felt life churning and spinning out of control. With this moment of time firmly planted in your mind, answer the following questions. Let's begin the journey of sitting quietly with your thoughts and strengthening your arsenal in Christ Jesus.

Many Blessings,

Crista

WHAT'S INSIDE?

1) There are eight chapters in *The Armor of God: Are You Sure You Got Dressed Today?* Each week the study will focus on one chapter in the book totaling an eight-week study.

2) The study includes five days of questions per week. Each day will contain one scripture for the day, three questions to answer, and a daily prayer to ask Jesus to cover and dress you in His armor to meet the day's challenges.

3) In place of some questions, you will **draw a picture**. Don't worry! My artistry rivals that of the stick-figure variety. Sometimes drawing just helps to solidify the concept in our mind a little better.

4) In place of some questions, you will complete a **word cloud**. For example, what words do you think of when you think of love?

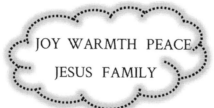

5) At the end of each chapter of questions, there is a place for you to write one or two things to share with the group and a place to jot down any notes.

May God bless you on your journey towards wrapping yourself in His perfect love and will for your life.

THE FULL ARMOR OF GOD

CHAPTER I

THE NAKED TRUTH

Finally, be strong in the Lord and in his mighty power. Put on the full armor of God, so that you can take your stand against the devil's schemes. For our struggle is not against flesh and blood, but against the rulers, against the authorities, against the powers of this dark world and against the spiritual forces of evil in the heavenly realms. Therefore put on the full armor of God, so that when the day of evil comes, you may be able to stand your ground, and after you have done everything, to stand.

—EPHESIANS 6:10–13 NIV

✣ DAY ONE ✣

"Jesus, wrap me in Your love and protection today."

1. What difficult time are you experiencing or have recently experienced?

_____

_____

_____

_____

_____

_____

_____

2. When things started to spin, did you feel in control of the situation or out of control? Why?

_____

_____

_____

_____

_____

_____

_____

_____

_____

3. When trials occur, do you feel close to God, mad at God, or think, *God who?* Explain.

_____

_____

_____

_____

_____

_____

_____

_____

_____

_____

MY DAILY PRAYER

Cast your cares on the LORD and he will sustain you; he will never let the righteous be shaken. —PSALM 55:22 NIV

Please share with God any experience, hurt, worry, anger, or fear that is burdening you today.

Dear Heavenly Father,

Right now, I give You what is on my heart:

_____

_____

_____

_____

_____

_____

While struggling with these trials, I ask that You put Your hand upon me. I need Your protection, guidance, and love. Hold my heart, my hand, and my circumstances as I lay them at the foot of the cross. I know You can lighten these burdens. Please give me a spirit of trust, so I can let go of the stronghold fear and worry have on me.

I know You are faithful, and You ask for my faith in return. I give it to You, Father. I give it all to You.

In Jesus' precious name I pray, Amen.

৯৯ DAY TWO ৯৯

"Jesus, wrap me in Your love and protection today."

SCRIPTURE FOR TODAY:

And let us not grow weary of doing good, for in due season we will reap, if we do not give up.

—GALATIANS 6:9 ESV

1. If you reached out to God during the stressful time you wrote about yesterday, did you feel comforted by Him? If so, how did you feel comforted?

_____

_____

_____

_____

_____

_____

_____

_____

2. Hindsight is always 20/20. Can you think of what choices, events, or circumstances were precursors to a recent struggle?

_____

_____

_____

_____

_____

_____

_____

_____

_____

_____

3. God welcomes our questions. List a few questions you would like God to answer about your trying situation.

_____

_____

_____

_____

_____

_____

_____

_____

_____

_____

MY DAILY PRAYER

Give all your worries and cares to God, for he cares about you.

—1 PETER 5:7 NLT

Please share with God any experience, hurt, worry, anger, or fear that is burdening you today.

Dear Heavenly Father,

Right now, I give You what is on my heart:

_____

_____

_____

_____

_____

_____

Help me to feel comforted by You, Lord. Let me know You are holding me in Your right hand and working all things together for my good.

Let me feel Your comfort and peace that surpasses all understanding and keep the enemy away from my thoughts of You. Please help me abandon my control of the situation and put it completely in Your hands. I know You can lighten what is burdening me.

Thank you for Your promises and for Your love that keeps and protects me from the evil one. I will seek You in everything that I do today.

In Jesus' precious name I pray, Amen.

⁓⁕⁓ DAY THREE ⁓⁕⁓

"Jesus, wrap me in Your love and protection today."

SCRIPTURE FOR TODAY:

When doubts filled my mind, your comfort gave me renewed hope and cheer.

—PSALM 94:19 NLT

1. Who or what are you relying on for protection? What makes this your protection of choice?

_____

_____

_____

_____

_____

_____

_____

_____

_____

2. Create a **word cloud** of what God's protection feels like.

3. The Bible says that God will never leave us nor forsake us. If this is true, why can it sometimes feel like He isn't present in our circumstances?

MY DAILY PRAYER

Lord, you have searched me and known me. You know when I sit down and when I stand up; you understand my thoughts from far away.

—PSALM 139:1–2 CSB

Please share with God any experience, hurt, worry, anger, or fear that is burdening you today.

Dear Heavenly Father,

Right now, I give You what is on my heart:

_____

_____

_____

_____

_____

_____

My precious Father, please help me to take the control out of my hands and dismiss the protections I surround myself with. Please gather me in Your arms today and teach my heart to rely solely upon Your provisions. Please help me to feel Your closeness as I go through my day.

Go before me Lord and pave the path You long for me to follow.

In Jesus' precious name I pray, Amen.

✐ DAY FOUR ✑

"Jesus, wrap me in Your love and protection today."

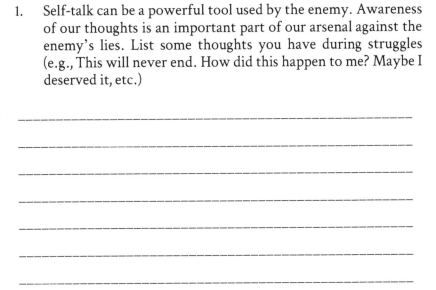

SCRIPTURE FOR TODAY:

"This is my command—be strong and courageous! Do not be afraid or discouraged. For the Lord your God is with you wherever you go."

—JOSHUA 1:9 NLT

1. Self-talk can be a powerful tool used by the enemy. Awareness of our thoughts is an important part of our arsenal against the enemy's lies. List some thoughts you have during struggles (e.g., This will never end. How did this happen to me? Maybe I deserved it, etc.)

_____

_____

_____

_____

_____

_____

_____

2. What bait is Satan using to lure you away from believing God's truths?

_____

_____

_____

_____

_____

_____

_____

_____

_____

3. What consistent patterns do you notice when Satan's lies snag you and you morph into that fish on a hook?

_____

_____

_____

_____

_____

_____

_____

_____

_____

_____

MY DAILY PRAYER

The Lord is my light and my salvation; whom shall I fear?

—PSALM 27:1 ESV

Please share with God any experience, hurt, worry, anger, or fear that is burdening you today.

Dear Heavenly Father,

Right now, I give You what is on my heart:

_____

_____

_____

_____

_____

_____

How blessed am I that You are all knowing and all powerful? Lord, You know the tactics the enemy uses to keep me flat on my back. Please give me the discernment to identify the bait Satan uses that stops me from running to You.

Lord, please help me to know the voice of the enemy. Empower me with the strength to muffle the lies that keep me from Your truths. I long to hear Your voice above the rest.

In Jesus' precious name I pray, Amen.

⚬⚬ DAY FIVE ⚬⚬

"Jesus, wrap me in Your love and protection today."

> SCRIPTURE FOR TODAY:
>
> *"I—yes, I alone—will blot out your sins for my own sake and will never think of them again."*
>
> —ISAIAH 43:25 NLT

1. Is there something in your life you feel God isn't willing to forgive? Are there things you can't forgive in yourself or in someone else? If Christ's sacrifice washes us clean, why is it unforgivable?

_____

_____

_____

_____

_____

_____

_____

_____

_____

2. Why do you think it's necessary to ask for God's armor daily? Why can't His armor be a one-stop-shop that upon asking, it will protect you for life?

_____

_____

_____

_____

_____

_____

_____

_____

3. What is something new you learned about yourself as you answered these questions?

_____

_____

_____

_____

_____

_____

_____

_____

Keep in mind the bait that Satan is using to entice you
away from God as you answer these questions.
Awareness of these arrows will free
you from their intended
STING.

MY DAILY PRAYER

"It is the Lord who goes before you. He will be with you; he will not leave you or forsake you. Do not fear or be dismayed."

—DEUTERONOMY 31:8 ESV

Please share with God any experience, hurt, worry, anger, or fear that is burdening you today.

Dear Heavenly Father,

Right now, I give You what is on my heart:

_____

_____

_____

_____

_____

_____

Your forgiveness is so humbling Lord. It is absolute and complete for all who come to You. Please give me a heart of forgiveness and shine light on the spots in my life where forgiveness is needed.

I need Your armor today, Lord. I need Your armor every day. It allows me to walk freely in a spiritual warzone because Your ways are perfect. You are perfect. Give me sight to see all You want me to know and understand and help open my heart allowing Your Spirit to flow through me today.

In Jesus' precious name I pray, Amen.

Sharing

Jot down a few thoughts from this week's lesson to
share with your group or with a friend.

_____
_____
_____
_____
_____
_____
_____
_____
_____

Notes

_____
_____
_____
_____
_____
_____
_____
_____
_____
_____
_____

THE BELT OF TRUTH

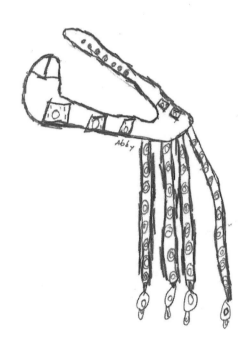

CHAPTER 2

THE MOST IMPORTANT ACCESSORY YOU WILL EVER OWN

Stand firm then, with the belt of truth buckled around your waist.

—EPHESIANS 6:14 NIV

◦৹৹ DAY ONE ৹৹◦

"Jesus, dress me in Your truth today."

1. Define the qualities you expect to see in a person who is truthful.

_____

_____

_____

_____

_____

_____

_____

_____

2.   Which of these qualities do you see in yourself?

_____

_____

_____

_____

_____

_____

_____

_____

_____

3.   Which qualities best define God?

_____

_____

_____

_____

_____

_____

_____

_____

_____

_____

_____

MY DAILY PRAYER

Blessed be the God and Father of our Lord Jesus Christ, the Father of mercies and God of all comfort.

—2 CORINTHIANS 1:3 NKJV

Please share with God any experience, hurt, worry, anger, or fear that is burdening you today.

Dear Heavenly Father,

Right now, I give You what is on my heart:

Jesus, You are the definition of truth. Help me to bring all my concerns and worries to the light of Your truth and chase away the shadows of the lies that hold me back.

Today help me to walk in Your truth, share Your truth, and taste the freedom of Your truth as I slip Your belt around my waist. It is by Your truth I am set free. Let me serve as Your vessel and shine the light on Your truths today.

In Jesus' precious name I pray, Amen.

✧ DAY TWO ✧

"Jesus, dress me in Your truth today."

> SCRIPTURE FOR TODAY:
>
> *Little children, let us not love in word or talk but in deed and in truth.*
>
> —1 JOHN 3:18 ESV

1. What negative thoughts about yourself is Satan using to snare you? When you bring forward these negative thoughts and hold them to the light of the Scriptures on the next page, you can see why Satan wants you deceived about who you really are in Christ.

_____

_____

_____

_____

_____

_____

_____

_____

"No, in all these things we are more than conquerors†
through him who loved us.† 38 For I am persuaded that
neither death nor life,† nor angels nor rulers,† nor things
present nor things to come,† nor powers, 39 nor height nor
depth, nor any other created thing will be able to separate
us from the love of God† that is in Christ Jesus our Lord."

—Romans 8:37–39 CSB

"For the Lord your God is living among you. He is a mighty
savior. He will take delight in you with gladness. With his
love, he will calm all your fears. He will rejoice over you
with joyful songs."

—Zephaniah 3:17 NLT

"I have been crucified with Christ and I no longer live, but
Christ lives in me. The life I now live in the body, I live by
faith in the Son of God, who loved me and gave himself for
me."

—Galatians 2:20 NIV

"For God so loved the world, that he gave his only begotten
Son, that whosoever believeth in him should not perish, but
have everlasting life."

—John 3:16 KJV

2. If these Scriptures say God loves and delights in you to the point He sacrificed His Son, then why continue to believe negative things about yourself? It is a struggle we all share. Are God's words truthful?

----

3. Create a **word cloud** by listing words from these Scriptures that tell how God sees you and how He shows His love for you.

MY DAILY PRAYER

When a man's ways please the LORD, he makes even his enemies to be at peace with him. —PROVERBS 16:7 ESV

Please share with God any experience, hurt, worry, anger, or fear that is burdening you today.

Dear Heavenly Father,

Right now, I give You what is on my heart:

_____

_____

_____

_____

_____

_____

There are times I choose to not walk in Your truth. I tend to believe the lies that try to define me. The truth is that You love me, You think I am beautiful and precious, and You died so I could live.

Please Lord, help me to tighten Your truth belt around my waist and feel Your truths wash over me. Help me to see all that You see in me, so I can grow and reflect the love of Christ.

In Jesus' precious name I pray, Amen.

✤ DAY THREE ✤

"Jesus, dress me in Your truth today."

SCRIPTURE FOR TODAY:

"God is spirit, and those who worship Him must worship in spirit and truth."

—JOHN 4:24 NASB

---

1. When things are going well, it is easy to believe God's protection is not needed. Describe how wearing His belt of truth is important even during the good times?

_____

_____

_____

_____

_____

_____

_____

_____

_____

2. What lie spoken by the enemy do you tend to listen to and
    believe the most? Why?

    ----

3. Can you think of someone in your life who would benefit from
    wearing God's truth belt? What lies can you see them listening
    to and believing?

MY DAILY PRAYER

I am not saying this because I am in need, for I have learned to be content whatever the circumstances.

—PHILIPPIANS 4:11 NIV

Please share with God any experience, hurt, worry, anger, or fear that is burdening you today.

Dear Heavenly Father,

Right now, I give You what is on my heart:

_____

_____

_____

_____

_____

_____

Lord, please never let me forget to wear Your armor of protection. I know the enemy uses the good times to help disarm what we believe is not needed. I am then headed for a trap I do not want to step into.

Help me to unpack the lies of the enemy today and discern what is true. Please allow my loved ones who are not walking in Your truth to hear and feel Your truths today. You can reach anyone anywhere. Please cover and protect those in my life that are lost.

In Jesus' precious name I pray, Amen.

৩৯ DAY FOUR ৯৩

"Jesus, dress me in Your truth today."

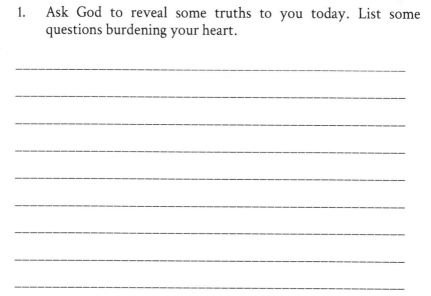

SCRIPTURE FOR TODAY:

In Him, you also, after listening to the message of truth, the gospel of your salvation—having also believed, you were sealed in Him with the Holy Spirit of promise.

—EPHESIANS 1:13 NASB

1. Ask God to reveal some truths to you today. List some questions burdening your heart.

_____

_____

_____

_____

_____

_____

_____

_____

_____

2. Write down what Jesus says in John 15:5.

_____

_____

_____

_____

_____

_____

3. To hear God's truths, John 15:5 says we need to remain connected to the vine of Jesus. **Draw a picture** of you connected to His vine.

MY DAILY PRAYER

But the Lord is faithful; he will strengthen you and guard you from the evil one. —2 THESSALONIANS 3:3 NLT

Please share with God any experience, hurt, worry, anger, or fear that is burdening you today.

Dear Heavenly Father,

Right now, I give You what is on my heart:

_____

_____

_____

_____

_____

_____

Connect me to Your vine, Jesus. Help me to flourish and grow in Your truths. When we are connected, the enemy cannot touch me.

When I wander Father, teach me how to return to You. Light the way and give me Your direction. Today, let me feel the strength and protection being close to You brings, Father. Outfit me with Your truths and open my ears to Your voice.

In Jesus' precious name I pray, Amen.

∾ DAY FIVE ∾

"Jesus, dress me in Your truth today."

SCRIPTURE FOR TODAY:

"If you abide In My word, you are My disciples indeed. And you shall know the truth, and the truth shall make you free."

—JOHN 8:31–32 NKJV

1. In your daily life, whose voice do you think you hear the most— yours, the enemy's, or God's? What makes you think so?

_____

_____

_____

_____

_____

_____

_____

_____

2. Is God sharing any truths with you today?

_____

_____

_____

_____

_____

_____

_____

_____

_____

_____

3. Which lies of the enemy are you ready to let go? (e.g., I can't do this, I am nobody, God can't fix this, etc.)

_____

_____

_____

_____

_____

_____

_____

_____

_____

_____

Below is some space for you to talk with God about your worries, concerns, frustrations, fears, and praises. God wants to hear all of it and writing it down is very cathartic. It's a release of control, so peace can seep in. Take a few minutes and spend some time with your Dad.

MY DAILY PRAYER

"You must not fear them, for the Lord your God Himself fights for you." —DEUTERONOMY 3:22 NKJV

Please share with God any experience, hurt, worry, anger, or fear that is burdening you today.

Dear Heavenly Father,

Right now, I give You what is on my heart:

_____

_____

_____

_____

_____

_____

You are my truth, Lord. You are my light. In Your hands I give You the contents of my heart: my joys, my fears, my worries, and my sorrows. I know You can handle it all, so I give it all over to You.

An emptiness falls over me, Lord, when my deaf ear is turned towards Your wisdom. When I ignore You, I am in a lonely place. When I believe the lies of the enemy, he entraps me in negative circumstances.

Allow me to hear Your truths today and take away the distractions. I give this day over to You, Lord. Do with it according to Your will.

In Jesus' precious name I pray, Amen.

<u>Sharing</u>

Jot down a few thoughts from this week's lesson to
share with your group or with a friend.

<u>Notes</u>

THE BREASTPLATE OF
RIGHTEOUSNESS

CHAPTER 3

I FEEL SO EXPOSED

With the breastplate of righteousness in place.

—EPHESIANS 6:14 NIV

༺ DAY ONE ༻

"Jesus, wrap me in Your righteousness today."

1. The same Satan that tricked Adam and Eve is the same Satan that tricks us today. It's easy to see how Adam and Eve fell for his lies, but why are we still falling for his lies today?

_____

_____

_____

_____

_____

_____

_____

_____

_____

2. How is feeling as protected from Satan's lies as a Roman soldier's chest is protected from spears change how you view your life? For example, does it build more confidence?

----

3. Create a **word cloud** by listing the surprise attacks Satan uses to snare us in our normal, everyday activities.

MY DAILY PRAYER

And the seed whose fruit is righteousness is sown in peace by those who make peace. —JAMES 3:18 NASB

Please share with God any experience, hurt, worry, anger, or fear that is burdening you today.

Dear Heavenly Father,

Right now, I give You what is on my heart:

_____

_____

_____

_____

_____

_____

How blessed are we that the rags of our own righteousness are not what You clothe us in. You made a way for us to wear Your pure and perfect righteousness. It is a gift beyond measure.

Protect my heart today from the enemy's flaming arrows. Let me suit up with Your perfect righteousness and make the enemy tremble. Let his lies fall to the ground as they miss their intended mark.

In Jesus' precious name I pray, Amen.

ꙮ DAY TWO ꙮ

"Jesus, wrap me in Your righteousness today."

SCRIPTURE FOR TODAY:

*God made him who had no sin to
be sin for us, so that in him we
might become the righteousness
of God.*

—2 CORINTHIANS 5:21 NIV

1. Jesus is a sinless man who died as if He sinned. Did someone
    ever unfairly blame you? Describe what happened.

_____

_____

_____

_____

_____

_____

_____

_____

2. During my trials, I struggled financially. A friend mailed a check out of the blue to help me pay my bills. This floored me. Did you ever receive an amazing gift you never expected? If so, describe the gift and how it made you feel?

----

3. Jesus' unfair death allows us to wear His breastplate of righteousness, so we can come before the Lord unblemished. How meaningful is this gift to you?

MY DAILY PRAYER

It is God who arms me with strength and keeps my way secure.

—PSALM 18:32 NIV

Please share with God any experience, hurt, worry, anger, or fear that is burdening you today.

Dear Heavenly Father,

Right now, I give You what is on my heart:

_____

_____

_____

_____

_____

_____

I am so undeserving of Your gift, Jesus. Help me to always stay humble and grateful for the protection You offer through Your death and resurrection. I need Your breastplate today, so I can walk a straight line and hear You with every step I take.

This is an unrepayable gift. Help me to use it wisely. Through my testimony and my walk with You, help me to point others to this gift so they inherit the same protection You freely offer me.

This is a gift that belongs not just to me. You gave it to us all.

In Jesus' precious name I pray, Amen.

ൟ DAY THREE ൟ

"Jesus, wrap me in Your righteousness today."

SCRIPTURE FOR TODAY:

But seek ye first the kingdom of God, and his righteousness; and all these things shall be added unto you.

—MATTHEW 6:33 KJV

1. Are your earbuds (life's distractions) allowing noise to drown out the voice of your Father who is trying to protect you? If so, once you remove the earbuds, what will He say about protecting your heart?

_____

_____

_____

_____

_____

_____

_____

_____

2. List some of life's distractions that keep your heart exposed.

_____

_____

_____

_____

_____

_____

_____

_____

_____

_____

3. How can wearing the righteousness of Christ help you focus more on His kingdom and less on your own.

_____

_____

_____

_____

_____

_____

_____

_____

_____

_____

_____

MY DAILY PRAYER

For You have armed me with strength for the battle; You have subdued under me those who rose up against me.

—PSALM 18:39 NKJV

Please share with God any experience, hurt, worry, anger, or fear that is burdening you today.

Dear Heavenly Father,

Right now, I give You what is on my heart:

_____

_____

_____

_____

_____

_____

Let my kingdom fall. Help me to walk over to Your kingdom and make my home with You. I allow so many things to divert my attention from You which guarantees I will remain unprotected in this spiritual battle. The flaming arrows hit their mark because my busyness keeps me from wearing Your breastplate.

Today let my eyes stop scanning the horizon and start looking up to meet Your gaze. I know You are with me. You are always with me. But Lord, I am not always with You. Help me walk closer to You today.

In Jesus' precious name I pray, Amen.

ஒ DAY FOUR ஒ

"Jesus, wrap me in Your righteousness today."

> SCRIPTURE FOR TODAY:
>
> *The eyes of the Lord are on the righteous, and His ears are open to their cry.*
>
> —PSALM 34:15 NKJV

1. Why is it so difficult for us to live a righteous life on our own?

_____
_____
_____
_____
_____
_____
_____
_____
_____
_____

2. Do you still feel earning righteousness is a way into heaven? Does the Bible say this is possible?

_____

_____

_____

_____

_____

_____

_____

_____

_____

3. Why is it so difficult for us to let go of our own righteousness and accept the perfect righteousness of Jesus?

_____

_____

_____

_____

_____

_____

_____

_____

_____

_____

MY DAILY PRAYER

Thus saith the Lord unto you, Be not afraid nor dismayed by reason of this great multitude; for the battle is not yours, but God's.

—2 CHRONICLES 20:15 KJV

Please share with God any experience, hurt, worry, anger, or fear that is burdening you today.

Dear Heavenly Father,

Right now, I give You what is on my heart:

_____

_____

_____

_____

_____

_____

Jesus, take away my aspirations to be greater than I am and stronger than I need to be. Change my desire to seek perfection in myself and those around me in this imperfect world.

You are the author of perfection. Yours is the righteousness I will never earn, live up to, or attain on my own abilities. Help me to bend my knees before You and acknowledge the holy gift You offer.

I am not perfect, Father. You know that, accept that, and love me endlessly anyway. Help me to forgive myself, forgive those around me, and lose my desire to earn what You won for me.

In Jesus' precious name I pray, Amen.

⊰ DAY FIVE ⊱

"Jesus, wrap me in Your righteousness today."

> SCRIPTURE FOR TODAY:
>
> *The wicked earns deceptive wages, but he who sows righteousness gets a true reward.*
>
> —PROVERBS 11:18 NASB

1. If you owned a piece of armor that protected a loved one's heart from Satan's attacks, who would you give it to and why?

_____

_____

_____

_____

_____

_____

_____

_____

_____

2. Sometimes the distractions and worries of this world start as soon as you open your eyes and your feet hit the ground. Why is taking time to pray for Christ's righteousness able to calm your nerves before you tackle the day?

_____

_____

_____

_____

_____

_____

_____

_____

_____

3. Is your heart as protected as your valuables? If your spiritual heart is a 4-carat diamond ring, what steps will you take to protect it?

_____

_____

_____

_____

_____

_____

_____

_____

_____

MY DAILY PRAYER

What then shall we say to these things? If God is for us, who is against us? —ROMANS 8:31 NASB

Please share with God any experience, hurt, worry, anger, or fear that is burdening you today.

Dear Heavenly Father,

Right now, I give You what is on my heart:

_____

_____

_____

_____

_____

_____

Today let my armor be complete. Please let Your righteousness fasten securely around my torso. This life isn't about me, Father. It is about You. I can't further Your kingdom if the enemy keeps me chasing the wind, and I keep forgetting who I am in You.

Help me to protect my heart, Father, and I pray for my friends and loved ones to feel secure in Your righteousness too. Let them know You more and give them a heart that seeks what only You can provide.

In Jesus' precious name I pray, Amen.

Sharing

Jot down a few thoughts from this week's lesson to
share with your group or with a friend.

_____

_____

_____

_____

_____

_____

_____

_____

Notes

_____

_____

_____

_____

_____

_____

_____

_____

_____

_____

THE SHOES OF PEACE

CHAPTER 4

MY ACHING FEET

And with your feet fitted with the readiness that comes from the gospel of peace.

—EPHESIANS 6:15 NIV

ᨏᨏ DAY ONE ᨏᨏ

"Jesus, slip Your shoes of peace on me today."

1. How many and what types of shoes do you own?

_____

_____

_____

_____

_____

_____

_____

_____

_____

2. Why did you choose to purchase these shoes? What purposes do they serve?

_____

_____

_____

_____

_____

_____

_____

_____

_____

3. How are Christ's shoes and your collection of shoes different?

_____

_____

_____

_____

_____

_____

_____

_____

MY DAILY PRAYER

"Blessed are the peacemakers, for they will be called children of God."
—MATTHEW 5:9 NASB

Please share with God any experience, hurt, worry, anger, or fear that is burdening you today.

Dear Heavenly Father,

Right now, I give You what is on my heart:

_____

_____

_____

_____

_____

_____

Lord, let my struggles be Yours. The only peace that can sustain me is Yours. Help me to seek only You and You alone. I have bought and tried many shoes in my life, but no shoe can do what Yours can.

Lord, help me to see what is needed to wear Your shoes. I find myself searching the world over for a joy that isn't there. Help me to stop, sit quietly with You, and allow Your peace to slip over me like a blanket. Calm my spirit today, Father. Help me rest in You.

In Jesus' precious name I pray, Amen.

૭ડ DAY TWO ຈ໑໐

"Jesus, slip Your shoes of peace on me today."

SCRIPTURE FOR TODAY:

Therefore being justified by faith,
we have peace with God through
our Lord Jesus Christ:

—ROMANS 5:1 KJV

1. Which pair of shoes did you spend more time on deciding to wear today—Christ's or yours? How much time did you spend on each of them?

_____

_____

_____

_____

_____

_____

_____

_____

2. **Draw a picture** of a pair of shoes providing you joy and peace no matter what may come.

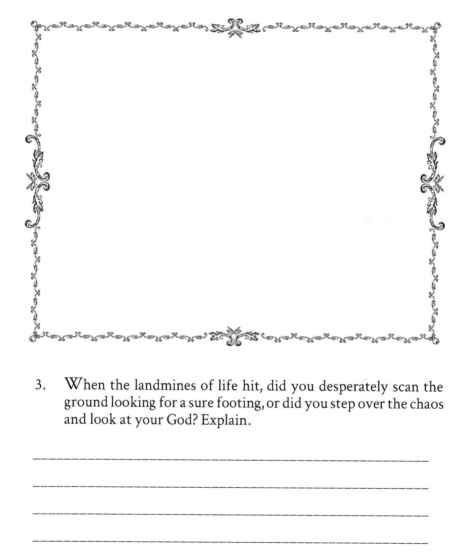

3. When the landmines of life hit, did you desperately scan the ground looking for a sure footing, or did you step over the chaos and look at your God? Explain.

_____

_____

_____

_____

_____

_____

_____

_____

MY DAILY PRAYER

I will give you thanks with all my heart; I will sing your praise before the heavenly beings. I will bow down toward your holy temple and give thanks to your name for your constant love and truth.

—PSALM 138:1–2 CSB

Please share with God any experience, hurt, worry, anger, or fear that is burdening you today.

Dear Heavenly Father,

Right now, I give You what is on my heart:

_____

_____

_____

_____

_____

_____

Lord, please help me to see peace in the chaos. When I see no way out, You are standing at the entrance of the door You are asking me to walk through. Help me to see it.

I know we were never meant to live in a perfect world. I spend so much time trying to avoid hurt and pain, that I begin taking control of my circumstances thinking I could somehow make it perfect.

Help me to find the joy and peace Your offer. It's a gift I don't open often enough.

In Jesus' precious name I pray, Amen.

ঙও DAY THREE ৩৯

"Jesus, slip Your shoes of peace on me today."

> SCRIPTURE FOR TODAY:
>
> *For Christ himself has brought peace to us. He united Jews and Gentiles into one people when, in his own body on the cross, he broke down the wall of hostility that separated us.*
>
> —EPHESIANS 2:14 NLT

1. Are you walking through life like the hero in the movie who is not distracted by the falling debris, or are you hiding—ducking and moving—during the difficult times? Explain.

_____

_____

_____

_____

_____

_____

_____

_____

2. If you did look to God to help you during this trial, describe how turning away from Him changes the way you handle this experience?

_____

_____

_____

_____

_____

_____

_____

_____

_____

3. Describe what living with peace and joy looks like even when things become difficult.

_____

_____

_____

_____

_____

_____

_____

_____

_____

_____

MY DAILY PRAYER

But thank God! He gives us victory over sin and death through our Lord Jesus Christ. —1 CORINTHIANS 15:57 NLT

Please share with God any experience, hurt, worry, anger, or fear that is burdening you today.

Dear Heavenly Father,

Right now, I give You what is on my heart:

Lord, teach me to see life through Your eyes. I give You all that is on my heart. I am tired of my peace being contingent on what is happening around me. Let my peace come directly from You.

I lift up my loved ones, Father. Let them feel Your unmistakable peace that has no beginning and no end. I want all of us to walk over our circumstances remembering they are temporary and not forever. Guide us to discern the lie that every valley is beyond Your reach.

In Jesus' precious name I pray, Amen.

৩৬ DAY FOUR ৩৬

"Jesus, slip Your shoes of peace on me today."

SCRIPTURE FOR TODAY:

The God of peace will soon crush Satan under your feet. May the grace of our Lord Jesus be with you.

—Romans 16:20 NLT

1. Does knowing that God is omnipresent, and His presence is with you always, bring you peace in your circumstances? Why or why not?

----

2. During your storms, what helpful reminders do you need to slip on Christ's shoes of peace?

_____

_____

_____

_____

_____

_____

_____

_____

_____

_____

3. List reasons someone is inclined to turn away from Christ's comfort and peace to handle the landmines on their own?

_____

_____

_____

_____

_____

_____

_____

_____

_____

_____

MY DAILY PRAYER

"Not by might nor by power, but by my Spirit," says the LORD Almighty. —ZECHARIAH 4:6 NIV

Please share with God any experience, hurt, worry, anger, or fear that is burdening you today.

Dear Heavenly Father,

Right now, I give You what is on my heart:

_____

_____

_____

_____

_____

_____

Jesus, You are the only way. You are my truth, and You are my light. Keep this truth at the forefront of my thoughts today. These are not my battles to win. They are Yours.

I pray for Your armor of protection to encapsulate me with Your love and mercy. I pray for those around me to see the gift I wear and have a curious heart as to where this incredible peace comes from. Give me the opportunity to point to You, Lord.

In Jesus' precious name I pray, Amen.

✤ DAY FIVE ✤

"Jesus, slip Your shoes of peace on me today."

> SCRIPTURE FOR TODAY:
>
> *Now may the Lord of peace Himself give you peace always in every way. The Lord be with you all.*
>
> —2 THESSALONIANS 3:16 NKJV

1. Are you in a place where you are out of a valley (loss, divorce, hurt, etc.) and able to guide someone else through a similar difficult time? List examples of you either wearing Christ's shoes of peace or stumbling through the situation by not wearing His shoes. Both examples are helpful to someone walking the same painful journey.

----

2. During a difficult time, who in your life benefits the most by observing you wearing Christ's shoes of peace? Why?

_____

_____

_____

_____

_____

_____

_____

_____

3. If Christ slipped His shoes of peace onto your feet right now, what changes would you expect to see and feel?

_____

_____

_____

_____

_____

_____

_____

_____

And the peace of God, which surpasses all understanding, will guard your hearts and your minds in Christ Jesus.

—Philippians 4:7 ESV

While on this side of the eternity equation, we are not meant to understand everything that occurs. His peace comes from a place beyond our imagination. It is a place where He holds our hearts and minds. We are always meant to look up. That is where our true home is, and that is where all understanding lies. While here, we are meant to exercise something called faith. It is through our faith that we remain humble and lean not on our own limited understanding. It is by faith that we freely slip on Christ's shoes and experience peace and joy in a world that sometimes doesn't make any sense.

Create a **word cloud** describing what Christ's
shoes of peace offer (e.g., freedom, no stress, light-weight, etc.).

MY DAILY PRAYER

Discretion will preserve you; Understanding will keep you.

—PROVERBS 2:11 NKJV

Please share with God any experience, hurt, worry, anger, or fear that is burdening you today.

Dear Heavenly Father,

Right now, I give You what is on my heart:

_____

_____

_____

_____

_____

_____

Lord, I thank You for the many valley's You guided me through. I know our stories are meant to be shared. Do You have someone in mind that I can help today? Help me to share the discernment You taught me and the understanding I gained during this difficult time.

During my trying times, please put people in my path who can hold my hand and walk me through as well. Help us to remind each other of Your peace and not be swept away by the winds that will come.

In Jesus' precious name I pray, Amen.

Sharing

Jot down a few thoughts from this week's lesson to
share with your group or with a friend.

Notes

THE SHIELD OF FAITH

CHAPTER 5

TO SHIELD OR NOT TO SHIELD

In addition to all of this, take up the shield of faith, with which you can extinguish all the flaming arrows of the evil one.

—EPHESIANS 6:16 NIV

✒ DAY ONE ✒

"Jesus, strengthen my faith and hope in You today."

1. What shields do you use daily to protect yourself from bad things that happen? (ex. vitamins to ward off illness, house for warmth, spouse to lean on, etc.)

_____

_____

_____

_____

_____

_____

_____

_____

2.   Have these shields ever failed you? What happened?

_____

_____

_____

_____

_____

_____

_____

_____

_____

_____

3.   Are you someone else's shield? If so, are you 100% effective? Explain.

_____

_____

_____

_____

_____

_____

_____

_____

_____

_____

MY DAILY PRAYER

Many are the afflictions of the righteous, but the LORD delivers him out of them all. —PSALM 34:19 ESV

Please share with God any experience, hurt, worry, anger, or fear that is burdening you today.

Dear Heavenly Father,

Right now, I give You what is on my heart:

_____

_____

_____

_____

_____

_____

Lord, why do I look everywhere but to You for protection? Help me to think of You as my first and only line of defense against the enemy's schemes. He is trying to derail me and those whom I love. Cover, protect, and guide us away from Satan's will and towards Your will, Jesus.

In this world, it is hard to let go of control. The enemy likes us to believe that we are in control, knowing full well we are not. This make us vulnerable. We need Your eyes to see, Lord. Help me to see today.

In Jesus' precious name I pray, Amen.

ɞɞ DAY TWO ɞɞ

"Jesus, strengthen my faith and hope in You today."

SCRIPTURE FOR TODAY:

"Go," said Jesus, "your faith has healed you." Immediately he received his sight and followed Jesus along the road.

—MARK 10:52 NIV

1. Do you describe yourself as a person who likes to feel in control of yourself and the world around you, or do you depend upon others or things to shield you from the storms? Give some examples of how you are one, the other, or both.

----

2. Why is putting your faith in your own abilities or someone else's abilities a possible letdown?

_____

_____

_____

_____

_____

_____

_____

_____

_____

_____

3. Do you think putting our faith in the Creator of the universe is 100% effective? Did God ever disappoint you? Explain.

_____

_____

_____

_____

_____

_____

_____

_____

_____

MY DAILY PRAYER

"The LORD will fight for you; you need only to be still."

—EXODUS 14:14 NIV

Please share with God any experience, hurt, worry, anger, or fear that is burdening you today.

Dear Heavenly Father,

Right now, I give You what is on my heart:

I lay my shields down before You, Lord. My created protection is broken in two. It is kindling at Your feet. Please help me to be vulnerable with You and teach my faith to strengthen only in Your love and protection, Lord.

I give You this day and every day. Break down what I hold up if it is not the shield of Your creation. Help me to guide others to the only shield that can take down the enemy's fiery darts.

In Jesus' precious name I pray, Amen.

➷ DAY THREE ➹

"Jesus, strengthen my faith and hope in You today."

SCRIPTURE FOR TODAY:

Now faith is the assurance of things hoped for, the conviction of things not seen.

—HEBREWS 11:1 NASB

1. How does carrying the shield of faith stop Satan's flaming arrows?

_____

_____

_____

_____

_____

_____

_____

_____

_____

2. Without Christ's shield, we spend our time trying to dodge the arrows that won't stop coming. It makes us stuck. Do you feel stuck in life or are you advancing forward? Why?

_____

_____

_____

_____

_____

_____

_____

_____

_____

3. If you feel stuck, what is keeping you planted where you stand?

_____

_____

_____

_____

_____

_____

_____

_____

_____

MY DAILY PRAYER

For I can do everything through Christ, who gives me strength.

—PHILIPPIANS 4:13 NLT

Please share with God any experience, hurt, worry, anger, or fear that is burdening you today.

Dear Heavenly Father,

Right now, I give You what is on my heart:

_____

_____

_____

_____

_____

_____

I can do all things through You. Your strength is enough, Your timing is perfect, and Your will is my path, even when I struggle to understand the *why*.

I get stuck in the fear, Lord. My shield is left at home and the arrows of doubt and worry once again capture my thoughts and feelings. Help me to remember to hold up Your shield daily and keep me advancing forward toward Your kingdom.

In Jesus' precious name I pray, Amen.

∘൭ DAY FOUR ൭∘

"Jesus, strengthen my faith and hope in You today."

> SCRIPTURE FOR TODAY:
>
> *"And whatever you ask in prayer, you will receive, if you have faith."*
>
> —MATTHEW 21:22 ESV

1. What do you rely upon to help you decrease anxiety and worry in your life? Is it working?

    _____

    _____

    _____

    _____

    _____

    _____

    _____

    _____

    _____

2. List ways to lay down the trust in yourself, others, or in the world and pick up God's shield of protection.

_____

_____

_____

_____

_____

_____

_____

_____

_____

_____

3. What happens if you pick up God's shield daily? Describe what this looks like as you go through a normal day.

_____

_____

_____

_____

_____

_____

_____

_____

_____

_____

MY DAILY PRAYER

You are my hiding place and my shield; I hope in Your word.

—PSALM 119:114 NKJV

Please share with God any experience, hurt, worry, anger, or fear that is burdening you today.

Dear Heavenly Father,

Right now, I give You what is on my heart:

_____

_____

_____

_____

_____

_____

Lord, thank You that even when I forget my shield, You are always willing to pick it up and put it back into my hand when I call upon You. You don't judge my weakened faith. Your only desire is that I step up, extend my hand, and take what You so freely give.

My faith is only made stronger in You. Apart from You, I am whisked in every direction. Help me to remain strong in faith, Lord. Help my faith to mature, grow, and spread.

In Jesus' precious name I pray, Amen.

ᴏᴈᴏ DAY FIVE ᴏᴈᴏ

"Jesus, strengthen my faith and hope in You today."

> SCRIPTURE FOR TODAY:
>
> *For we walk by faith, not by sight.*
>
> —2 CORINTHIANS 5:7 ESV

1. What comes to mind when you think about Christ's shield of faith?

_____

_____

_____

_____

_____

_____

_____

_____

_____

2. Are you facing any giants today?

_____

_____

_____

_____

_____

_____

_____

_____

_____

_____

3. How does your faith shield protect and keep you advancing forward despite any arrow—big or small—aimed at your heart?

_____

_____

_____

_____

_____

_____

_____

_____

_____

_____

_____

O nce you put down your own shield and pick up God's faith shield, you grow in trust and strength as you experience the power and protection of God. This makes it easier to pick up and hold His shield against the next arrows that fall—because the arrows will always fall. God loves you and wants to shield you. He invites you to test the validity and durability of His shield. He is your Dad, and you are His child. As you leave to go about your day, His shield is waiting for you to pick up by the front door.

Inside of the frame, **draw a picture** of yourself holding the shield of faith thwarting Satan's arrows.

MY DAILY PRAYER

Keep thy heart with all diligence; for out of it are the issues of life.

—PROVERBS 4:23 KJV

Please share with God any experience, hurt, worry, anger, or fear that is burdening you today.

Dear Heavenly Father,

Right now, I give You what is on my heart:

_____

_____

_____

_____

_____

_____

The arrows are coming, the giants are advancing forward, and I feel so small sometimes, Lord. Expand my shield to cover all that forms against my family and me.

Lord, help me to step out in faith even when unknown giants are looming, and the flaming arrows are blinding my sight. I only need to rely on Your eyes to see and Your voice to speak, so I can follow where You want me to go today.

In Jesus' precious name I pray, Amen.

Sharing

Jot down a few thoughts from this week's lesson to
share with your group or with a friend.

_____

_____

_____

_____

_____

_____

_____

_____

_____

Notes

_____

_____

_____

_____

_____

_____

_____

_____

_____

THE HELMET OF SALVATION

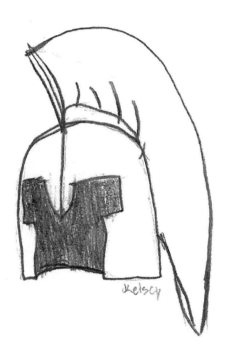

CHAPTER 6

ALWAYS WEAR YOUR HELMET!

Take the helmet of salvation.

—EPHESIANS 6:17 NIV

৩৬ DAY ONE ৩৩

"Jesus, cover me with Your grace and mercy today."

1. Describe some beautiful experiences that you've had in this world (experiences in nature, with family, hope, etc.).

_____

_____

_____

_____

_____

_____

_____

_____

2. If God is the author of beauty, kindness, love, sacrifice, and forgiveness, what beautiful things from your list would leave if God left us? Why?

    _____

    _____

    _____

    _____

    _____

    _____

    _____

    _____

    _____

    _____

3. Create a **word cloud** of what saved by grace means to you.

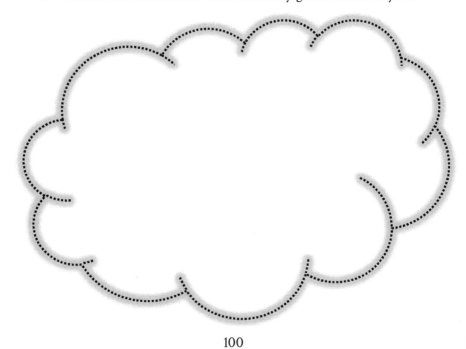

MY DAILY PRAYER

For who is God except the LORD? Who but our God is a solid rock?

—2 SAMUEL 22:32 NLT

Please share with God any experience, hurt, worry, anger, or fear that is burdening you today.

Dear Heavenly Father,

Right now, I give You what is on my heart:

_____

_____

_____

_____

_____

_____

Your sacrifice is so humbling, Lord. At times, I don't understand it. Other times, I question it. Right now, I need to believe in it.

You are the Creator over all. You sacrificed so I can live in an eternity with the maker of heaven and Earth. Forever, because of your grace, I can experience all the beauty You created. I am in awe today, Lord. Avert my eyes and attention away from my worries and cares and shift it towards the beauty of Your love and sacrifice.

In Jesus' precious name I pray, Amen.

✎ DAY TWO ✎

"Jesus, cover me with Your grace and mercy today."

> SCRIPTURE FOR TODAY:
>
> *For by grace you have been saved through faith. And this is not your own doing; it is the gift of God, not a result of works, so that no one may boast.*
>
> —EPHESIANS 2:8–9 ESV

1. Do you believe you need to be good enough to enter heaven? Why or why not?

_____

_____

_____

_____

_____

_____

_____

_____

2. If your sin is *big* enough, do you believe it is possible to lose your salvation?

_____

_____

_____

_____

_____

_____

_____

_____

_____

_____

3. How does life change if God decided against sending His Son to die for your sins, and you had to earn your way into heaven?

_____

_____

_____

_____

_____

_____

_____

_____

_____

_____

MY DAILY PRAYER

The name of the LORD is a strong tower; The righteous runs into it and is safe. —PROVERBS 18:10 NASB

Please share with God any experience, hurt, worry, anger, or fear that is burdening you today.

Dear Heavenly Father,

Right now, I give You what is on my heart:

_____

_____

_____

_____

_____

_____

Lord, thank You so much for the ultimate gift. Because You chose to lose Your life, I can now live mine. I am so grateful my future allows me to spend my eternity with You, Father.

I never want to forget Your sacrifice or take it for granted. I can't imagine sending my son or daughter to do what You did for humanity. I know I continue to break Your heart. I am grateful to You for loving me so much anyway. Let me follow Your example of grace and forgiveness today.

In Jesus' precious name I pray, Amen.

∾ DAY THREE ∾

"Jesus, cover me with Your grace and mercy today."

> ### SCRIPTURE FOR TODAY:
>
> *For one will scarcely die for a righteous person—though perhaps for a good person one would dare even to die— but God shows his love for us in that while we were still sinners, Christ died for us.*
>
> —ROMANS 5:7–8 ESV

1. Do you think some people still believe in earning salvation? If so, why do you think they believe this?

_____

_____

_____

_____

_____

_____

_____

_____

2. Is it easy or difficult for you to believe that Christ died for your sins? Explain.

_____

_____

_____

_____

_____

_____

_____

_____

3. Because Jesus died and rose from the dead, we are gifted a clean bill of health. We are born again. Why is spiritual rebirth so important to God?

_____

_____

_____

_____

_____

_____

_____

_____

MY DAILY PRAYER

The LORD is good, A stronghold in the day of trouble; And He knows those who trust in Him.

—NAHUM 1:7 NKJV

Please share with God any experience, hurt, worry, anger, or fear that is burdening you today.

Dear Heavenly Father,

Right now, I give You what is on my heart:

_____

_____

_____

_____

_____

_____

I give my life over to You today, Lord. You lost your life, so I could gain mine. I owe You so much more than merely just existing. I owe a life that is pleasing and honoring to You.

I will falter and fail as I try to do this, Lord. Please hold me up and remind me Your sacrifice covers even this. Let me not give to You out of duty, but out of love. Teach me how I can sacrifice for You today.

In Jesus' precious name I pray, Amen.

❧ DAY FOUR ☙

"Jesus, cover me with Your grace and mercy today."

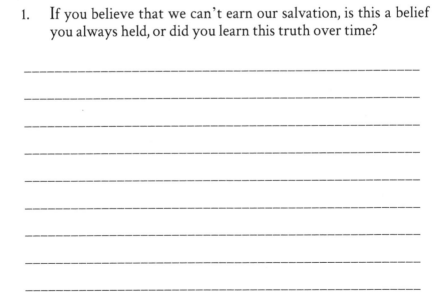

SCRIPTURE FOR TODAY:

You, dear children, are from God and have overcome them, because the one who is in you is greater than the one who is in the world.

—1 JOHN 4:4 NIV

1. If you believe that we can't earn our salvation, is this a belief you always held, or did you learn this truth over time?

_____

_____

_____

_____

_____

_____

_____

_____

2. If we are sinners and unworthy of His sacrifice, why did Jesus
    decide to go through such a horrible death for us?

_____

_____

_____

_____

_____

_____

_____

_____

_____

3. God said that sin's punishment is an eternal separation from
    Him. Why isn't living a good life enough? Is it mandatory to
    accept Christ's sacrifice?

_____

_____

_____

_____

_____

_____

_____

_____

_____

MY DAILY PRAYER

And lead us not into temptation, but deliver us from evil: For thine is the kingdom, and the power, and the glory, for ever. Amen.

—MATTHEW 6:13 KJV

Please share with God any experience, hurt, worry, anger, or fear that is burdening you today.

Dear Heavenly Father,

Right now, I give You what is on my heart:

_____

_____

_____

_____

_____

_____

Lord, I lay at Your feet the hearts and souls of those around me who are not yet saved. Give me a heart to help and an opportunity to guide them to You. Even in my own struggles, I choose to advance Your kingdom—not mine. You gave me everything. I want to give back.

I am Your number one sinner, Lord. I wonder how You continue to love me sometimes. Help me to see what You see in me. Help me to find the light within that You lit for all to see. Help me dust off the sins that You forgave. Use me today, Lord. Let me be Your light.

In Jesus' precious name I pray, Amen.

∂ DAY FIVE ∂

"Jesus, cover me with Your grace and mercy today."

> SCRIPTURE FOR TODAY:
>
> *"Nor is there salvation in any other, for there is no other name under heaven given among men by which we must be saved."*
>
> —ACTS 4:12 NKJV

1. Since God allowed His son to die for us, what does that say about God?

_____

_____

_____

_____

_____

_____

_____

_____

2. Who is in your prayers right now who doesn't know or believe in the freeing sacrifice of Jesus Christ?

_____

_____

_____

_____

_____

_____

_____

_____

_____

3. If you could sit them in front of you right now, what truths about Jesus' sacrifice would you like them to know? If this is you, what questions do you need answered before you are willing to accept the sacrifice He made out of love for you?

_____

_____

_____

_____

_____

_____

_____

_____

_____

_____

Now it was about the sixth hour, and there was darkness over all the earth until the ninth hour. Then the sun was darkened, and the veil of the temple was torn in two. And when Jesus had cried out with a loud voice, He said, "Father, 'into Your hands I commit My spirit.'" Having said this, He breathed His last.

—LUKE 23:44–46 NKJV

Draw a picture of the scene described in these verses.

MY DAILY PRAYER

He guards the paths of the just and protects those who are faithful to him. —PROVERBS 2:8 NLT

Please share with God any experience, hurt, worry, anger, or fear that is burdening you today.

Dear Heavenly Father,

Right now, I give You what is on my heart:

_____

_____

_____

_____

_____

_____

Lord, I lift my loved ones to You. Some are still choosing to live in the veil of darkness. They think they are in the light, but it is a false light.

Put me in the path of those I love and let them see Your light in me. Surround them with coworkers, chance meetings with strangers, and anyone else who can be a link in the chain of their unbelief. Let these collective lights cut through their darkness, so they truly can believe.

Please lift off the blindfolds of the enemy, and let my loved ones know and accept Your sacrifice. These are Your children, Father, and I know You love them more than I ever could.

In Jesus' precious name I pray, Amen.

Sharing

Jot down a few thoughts from this week's lesson to
share with your group or with a friend.

_____

_____

_____

_____

_____

_____

_____

_____

_____

Notes

_____

_____

_____

_____

_____

_____

_____

_____

_____

_____

THE SWORD OF THE SPIRIT

CHAPTER 7

"TAKE THAT!"

And the sword of the Spirit, which is the word of God.

—EPHESIANS 6:17 NIV

∞ **DAY ONE** ∞

"Jesus, let Your Word wash over me today."

1. Who introduced you to the Bible? How old were you?

_____

_____

_____

_____

_____

_____

_____

_____

_____

_____

2.   The Bible is a powerful sword with wisdom for everyday life questions. What questions do you need the Bible to answer for you today?

_____

_____

_____

_____

_____

_____

_____

_____

_____

3.   On a scale of 1-10 (ten is the highest), how intimidating is it for you to read the Bible? Why?

_____

_____

_____

_____

_____

_____

_____

_____

MY DAILY PRAYER

"I will refresh the weary and satisfy the faint."

—JEREMIAH 31:25 NIV

Please share with God any experience, hurt, worry, anger, or fear that is burdening you today.

Dear Heavenly Father,

Right now, I give You what is on my heart:

_____

_____

_____

_____

_____

_____

Let Your Word be on my lips today, Father. Let my sword be ready for the draw as the enemy attempts to thwart Your plans. Help me to live according to Your Word and give me the wisdom to understand its meaning.

I pray for a willing spirit to open You precious book. Guide me to the right passage that You want spoken into my life today.

In Jesus' precious name I pray, Amen.

๑๑ DAY TWO ๑๑

"Jesus, let Your Word wash over me today."

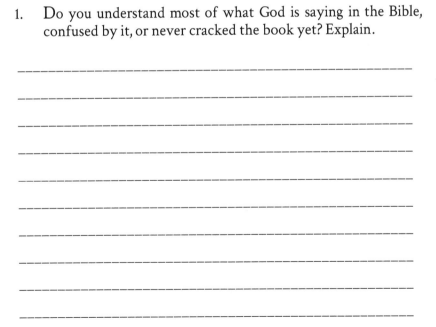

SCRIPTURE FOR TODAY:

"The grass withers, the flower fades, but the word of our God stands forever."

—ISAIAH 40:8 NKJV

1. Do you understand most of what God is saying in the Bible, confused by it, or never cracked the book yet? Explain.

_____

_____

_____

_____

_____

_____

_____

_____

_____

2.   If you are a regular reader, how often do you open God's Word?
     What routine did you set into place?

----

3.   How often do life's demands keep you from reading His Word?
     List some distractions that come your way.

When you become aware of what is distracting you from
reading God's Word, you are able to pinpoint the
pattern of arrows Satan uses to guarantee the Word of God
remains closed. Learn these patterns and fight back!

MY DAILY PRAYER

When I am afraid, I put my trust in you.

—PSALM 56:3 ESV

Please share with God any experience, hurt, worry, anger, or fear that is burdening you today.

Dear Heavenly Father,

Right now, I give You what is on my heart:

_____

_____

_____

_____

_____

_____

Lord, why do I worry and fear so much when Your Word tells me not to? Your Word is alive and active, yet I struggle sometimes to let it cultivate in my heart.

In Your Word, You promise to give me rest. You say You will take down my enemies and cover me with Your love. Your Word has a lot to say about my life. Give me eyes to see and ears to hear all that You are trying to tell me, Lord. Let Your Word guide my steps each day.

In Jesus' precious name I pray, Amen.

⚬⚬ DAY THREE ⚬⚬

"Jesus, let Your Word wash over me today."

> SCRIPTURE FOR TODAY:
>
> *In the beginning was the Word,*
> *and the Word was with God, and*
> *the Word was God.*
>
> —JOHN 1:1 KJV

1. If life is so busy, how is it possible that stopping and reading the Bible adds more time to your day?

_____

_____

_____

_____

_____

_____

_____

_____

_____

2. If you feel comfortable reading God's Word, what wisdom would you offer to someone who is uncomfortable reading the Bible?

    _____

    _____

    _____

    _____

    _____

    _____

    _____

    _____

    _____

3. Do you believe the Bible is the inspired Word of God? Explain.

    _____

    _____

    _____

    _____

    _____

    _____

    _____

    _____

    _____

MY DAILY PRAYER

Commit your works to the LORD
And your plans will be established.

—PROVERBS 16:3 NASB

Please share with God any experience, hurt, worry, anger, or fear that is burdening you today.

Dear Heavenly Father,

Right now, I give You what is on my heart:

_____

_____

_____

_____

_____

_____

Lord, my days and nights are running together. I am lost and chasing shadows. Your Word is the light to my path. Help me to open it faithfully. Help me to sharpen my sword.

Lord, provide opportunities to share Your Word with others. Give me a strong understanding of the Bible, so I can pass this knowledge to those around me. Help my sword to sharpen theirs, and their sword to sharpen mine.

In Jesus' precious name I pray, Amen.

◈ DAY FOUR ◈

"Jesus, let Your Word wash over me today."

> SCRIPTURE FOR TODAY:
>
> *For the word of God is alive and powerful. It is sharper than the sharpest two-edged sword, cutting between soul and spirit, between joint and marrow. It exposes our innermost thoughts and desires.*
>
> —HEBREWS 4:12 NLT

1. Why is Satan fearful of God's Word? How do you know that he fears it?

_____

_____

_____

_____

_____

_____

_____

_____

2. How is it possible that the Bible is active, alive, and relevant? Isn't it just too old?

_____

_____

_____

_____

_____

_____

_____

_____

_____

3. Why is it important for you to read the Bible and come to your own conclusions? Why not just trust what someone else is telling you about His Word?

_____

_____

_____

_____

_____

_____

_____

_____

_____

MY DAILY PRAYER

And this is the confidence that we have toward him, that if we ask anything according to his will he hears us.

—1 JOHN 5:14 ESV

Please share with God any experience, hurt, worry, anger, or fear that is burdening you today.

Dear Heavenly Father,

Right now, I give You what is on my heart:

_____

_____

_____

_____

_____

_____

Lord, give me Your wisdom and understanding as I enter into Your Word. Protect me from Satan who tempts me to close Your Word and focus to my many distractions.

Satan knows the power Your Word holds. If he understands the strength in Your Word, then how much more should I? You gave me this offensive tool to protect me from harm, to fight against the enemy's attacks, and keep him running in the opposite direction. Remind me daily not leave my home without this mighty blade.

In Jesus' precious name I pray, Amen.

⊶⊷ DAY FIVE ⊷⊶

"Jesus, let Your Word wash over me today."

SCRIPTURE FOR TODAY:

"Every word of God is flawless; he is a shield to those who take refuge in him."

—PROVERBS 30:5 NIV

1. What misconceptions do people have about the Bible? Did you have any of these misconceptions before you read His Word?

_____

_____

_____

_____

_____

_____

_____

_____

_____

_____

2.   Do you believe the Bible's purpose is to make you feel guilty by pointing out what you are doing wrong? If so, why?

_____

_____

_____

_____

_____

_____

_____

_____

_____

_____

3.   Create a **word cloud** describing what it means to trust in the Word of God.

The Word became flesh and made his dwelling among us.
We have seen his glory, the glory of the one and only Son,
who came from the Father, full of grace and truth.

—JOHN 1:14 NIV

The Word became flesh in Jesus, and He is our sword. Amen!
Draw what it looks like wielding your sword and fighting against
the enemy's lies.

MY DAILY PRAYER

LORD, hear my prayer, listen to my cry for mercy; in your faithfulness and righteousness come to my relief.

—PSALM 143:1 NIV

Please share with God any experience, hurt, worry, anger, or fear that is burdening you today.

Dear Heavenly Father,

Right now, I give You what is on my heart:

_____

_____

_____

_____

_____

_____

Lord, I desire to be Your sword-wielding soldier. I long to fight and win against the enemy who relentlessly attacks us. I don't want to merely survive his tricks and lies, I want them to never have a foothold in my life.

Teach me, Father, to rely solely on Your Word as my offensive weapon. Help me to carve out time and stick to a reading plan that keeps my sword strong and my enemy scared.

In Jesus' precious name I pray, Amen.

Sharing

Jot down a few thoughts from this week's lesson to
share with your group or with a friend.

_____

_____

_____

_____

_____

_____

_____

_____

_____

Notes

_____

_____

_____

_____

_____

_____

_____

_____

_____

_____

_____

THE WAR IS WON

CHAPTER 8

ARE YOU DRESSED FOR SUCCESS?

For although we live in the flesh, we do not wage war according
to the flesh, since the weapons of our warfare are not of the flesh,
but are powerful through God for the demolition of strongholds.
We demolish arguments and every proud thing that is raised up
against the knowledge of God, and we take every thought captive
to obey Christ.

—2 CORINTHIANS 10:3–5 CSB

∽ DAY ONE ∾

"Jesus, I lay my life at Your feet today."

1. How often in your life do you leave your home without God's
   armor of protection? How do you know you're not protected?

----

2. Turning back time, what one experience would change drastically if you suited up with God's protection?

_____

_____

_____

_____

_____

_____

_____

_____

_____

3. Knowing that Satan uses our busy lives to distract us from clothing ourselves in God's armor, how can you plan for this and make time to pray, read God's Word, and sit quietly with Him?

_____

_____

_____

_____

_____

_____

_____

_____

_____

MY DAILY PRAYER

Let me hear in the morning of your steadfast love, for in you I trust.
Make me know the way I should go, for to you I lift up my soul.

—PSALM 143:8 ESV

Please share with God any experience, hurt, worry, anger, or fear that is burdening you today.

Dear Heavenly Father,

Right now, I give You what is on my heart:

_____

_____

_____

_____

_____

_____

Lord, I want to live in the truth that the war is won. I am living my eternity with You now, and nothing that Satan tries to do will snatch me from Your hands. Why do I fear? Why do I worry? Why do I live as if the future is unknown?

We are victors in Christ. We can carry the banner of our eternity with Him, yet the enemy tries to make me believe that I am still lost.

The war is won, Father. Help me to live my life in this truth.

In Jesus' precious name I pray, Amen.

◈ DAY TWO ◈

"Jesus, I lay my life at Your feet today."

SCRIPTURE FOR TODAY:

It is clear evidence of God's righteous judgment that you will be counted worthy of God's kingdom, for which you also are suffering.

—2 THESSALONIANS 1:5 CSB

1. If you could build your own kingdom on this Earth, describe how it looks and functions.

_____

_____

_____

_____

_____

_____

_____

_____

2. Compare this earthly kingdom with God's kingdom. What similarities and differences do you see between these two kingdoms?

_____

_____

_____

_____

_____

_____

_____

_____

_____

_____

3. Why is it so easy for Satan to convince us to focus so much of our time and attention on our earthly home at the expense of our heavenly home?

_____

_____

_____

_____

_____

_____

_____

_____

_____

MY DAILY PRAYER

The LORD is near to all who call upon Him, to all who call upon Him in truth. —PSALM 145:18 NKJV

Please share with God any experience, hurt, worry, anger, or fear that is burdening you today.

Dear Heavenly Father,

Right now, I give You what is on my heart:

_____

_____

_____

_____

_____

_____

Lord, I pray my attention is focused on You today. I have given so much of my time and energy to things that don't matter, aren't forever, or were never meant to be my burden to carry. I desire, Lord, to seek Your kingdom above my own.

Give me a heart of understanding when my focus is away from You and on my own kingdom. I need Your reminders that my kingdom is temporary and Yours is the everlasting truth.

In Jesus' precious name I pray, Amen.

❧ DAY THREE ❧

"Jesus, I lay my life at Your feet today."

> SCRIPTURE FOR TODAY:
>
> *"I have told you these things so that in me you may have peace. You will have suffering in this world. Be courageous! I have conquered the world."*
>
> —JOHN 16:33 CSB

1. Satan fears you putting on God's armor. Why?

_____

_____

_____

_____

_____

_____

_____

_____

_____

2. List some reasons why a person may choose to not wear God's armor every day.

_____

_____

_____

_____

_____

_____

_____

_____

_____

3. Do you pay more attention to your physical needs or your spiritual health? How do you know?

_____

_____

_____

_____

_____

_____

_____

_____

_____

MY DAILY PRAYER

But my God shall supply all your need according to his riches in glory by Christ Jesus. —PHILIPPIANS 4:19 KJV

Please share with God any experience, hurt, worry, anger, or fear that is burdening you today.

Dear Heavenly Father,

Right now, I give You what is on my heart:

_____

_____

_____

_____

_____

_____

Thank You, Lord, for being at the beginning and the ending of my life. Thank You for wanting to be in even the smallest of details. This creates a stronger relationship with You. I can't imagine how different my life would be if I was left alone to fend for myself.

Lord, You won this war for me. You won this war for all who wish to seek and find You, Your kingdom, and eternal life with You. Help me to live in such a way that others notice and ask about my peace and joy. Let everything I do always point back to You.

In Jesus' precious name I pray, Amen.

๑๑ DAY FOUR ๑๑

"Jesus, I lay my life at Your feet today."

> SCRIPTURE FOR TODAY:
>
> *God is our refuge and strength, an ever-present help in trouble.*
>
> —Psalm 46:1 NIV

1. If Christ sat down next to you right now and asked, "Did you live today for Me, or did you live today for you?" how would you answer Him?

_____

_____

_____

_____

_____

_____

_____

_____

2. In what ways can we live each day for Christ? Do they need to be big things to count?

_____

_____

_____

_____

_____

_____

_____

_____

_____

_____

3. If God holds even the smallest life in His hands, how important do you think you are to God? Why?

_____

_____

_____

_____

_____

_____

_____

_____

_____

_____

_____

MY DAILY PRAYER

And so we know and rely on the love God has for us. God is love.
Whoever lives in love lives in God, and God in them.

—1 JOHN 4:16 NIV

Please share with God any experience, hurt, worry, anger, or fear that is burdening you today.

Dear Heavenly Father,

Right now, I give You what is on my heart:

_____

_____

_____

_____

_____

_____

Lord, You are in the smallest details. Nothing escapes Your attention. Every tear I cry, You wipe away. Every fear I have, You are holding my hand. Every worry I carry, You ask me to lay them at Your feet. Help me to always be aware of how much I matter to You.

The enemy chooses to keep fighting a war that he has already lost. Please give me the childlike faith needed to bring him down. Grant me a willing spirit, a trusting heart, and a bubbling joy like a child following their Dad wherever He goes.

In Jesus' precious name I pray, Amen.

◦◦◦ DAY FIVE ◦◦◦

"Jesus, I lay my life at Your feet today."

> SCRIPTURE FOR TODAY:
>
> *Therefore I will look unto the LORD; I will wait for the God of my salvation: my God will hear me.*
>
> —MICAH 7:7 KJV

1. Do you, or someone you know, blame God for the evil in this world? Is it fair to blame Him? Why or why not?

----

2. God's original plan involved a world of peace without death or sin. When bad things happen, is knowing that our sinful world was not part of His original design helpful? Why or why not?

_____

_____

_____

_____

_____

_____

_____

_____

_____

3. The Roman soldiers connected their shields in battle to create a more effective protective barrier. If the armor of God scripture is a battle cry, describe the changes in your home, work, community, or world that would take place if you connected your faith shield with other believers.

_____

_____

_____

_____

_____

_____

_____

_____

The War Is Already Won!

Saturday evening, when the Sabbath ended, Mary Magdalene, Mary the mother of James, and Salome went out and purchased burial spices so they could anoint Jesus' body. Very early on Sunday morning, just at sunrise, they went to the tomb. On the way they were asking each other, "Who will roll away the stone for us from the entrance to the tomb?" But as they arrived, they looked up and saw that the stone, which was very large, had already been rolled aside.

When they entered the tomb, they saw a young man clothed in a white robe sitting on the right side. The women were shocked, but the angel said, "Don't be alarmed. You are looking for Jesus of Nazareth, who was crucified. He isn't here! He is risen from the dead! Look, this is where they laid his body. Now go and tell his disciples, including Peter, that Jesus is going ahead of you to Galilee. You will see him there, just as he told you before he died."

—MARK 16: 1–7 NLT

Create a word cloud of your thoughts on these verses.

MY DAILY PRAYER

"Let not your heart be troubled; you believe in God, believe also in Me." —JOHN 14:1 NKJV

Please share with God any experience, hurt, worry, anger, or fear that is burdening you today.

Dear Heavenly Father,

Right now, I give You what is on my heart:

_____
_____
_____
_____
_____
_____

I believe in You, Lord. I believe You won this war the second You breathed Your last breath. Your sacrifice brings me to my knees. May I always remember what You did for me.

Lord, we continue to be in dark times. The enemy wants us to not believe in Your sovereignty but in his. Help me find others to connect my faith shield, so we can advance forward for Your kingdom. Help us to win the hearts Satan is trying to snatch away from You. Give us the opportunity to point others to the war You have already won.

In Jesus' precious name I pray, Amen.

The tomb is empty. You have a choice to make. Do you believe that Jesus rose from the dead, do you run in fright, or do you go and tell everyone you know and love? The war is won, but Satan insists he is in control and possesses a chance to win. At least that is what he wants *you* to think.

He attempts to spin the lie that the empty tomb does not mean his time to wreak havoc on this Earth, and in your life, is limited. His only way in succeeding at keeping you away from the truth is by convincing you to stay naked and vulnerable.

You have a choice as to whether you believe Jesus already won this war. He loves you so much that He died to give you this choice. Your armor is waiting.

What will you decide to wear today?

Sharing

Jot down a few thoughts from this week's lesson to
share with your group or with a friend.

Notes

GROUP BIBLE STUDY
SPECIAL PRICING

The Armor of God

The Workbook Companion for The Armor of God

Please contact me here:

cristacrawford.com/contact

NEWSLETTER

Sign up to receive a ***once a month*** newsletter full of updates on new book releases, giveaways, discounts, and encouragement.

Sign up here:

cristacrawford.com/newsletter

ABOUT THE AUTHOR

Crista Crawford is an imperfect Christian writing about her perfect God. She discovered the power of praying each piece of armor into her life after stumbling through multiple trials only to fall face-first without it.

Crista is a wife, mother, and stepmother who feels incredibly blessed sharing life with these amazing people. She is an Emerson Excellence in Teaching Award winner and has a Master of Science in Speech-Language Pathology and a Master of Arts in Educational studies with Reading Emphasis. She has over twenty years' experience as a Speech-Language Pathologist and forty-plus years learning what grace and forgiveness really mean.

Please visit Crista on Goodreads, Amazon, or Barnes and Noble and let her know your thoughts on *The Full Armor of God* and *The Workbook Companion for The Full Armor of God.* Any thoughts are greatly appreciated!

We are meant to share our testimonies to light the path for those who still struggle in the dark. What we overcome is the very foundation for others to use as their stepping stone.

Connect with Crista!

Website: cristacrawford.com
Facebook: facebook.com/CCrawfordAuthor
Twitter: @CCrawfordAuthor
Instagram: instagram.com/ccrawfordauthor
Goodreads: bit.ly/cristacrawford

Made in the USA
Middletown, DE
30 December 2022

20754318R00097